P9-CND-670

This Item is no longer property
of Pima County Public Library
Sale of this item benefited the Libra

HIPPOPOTAMUSES

by Josh Gregory

Children's Press®

An Imprint of Scholastic Inc.

Content Consultant
Dr. Stephen S. Ditchkoff
Professor of Wildlife Ecology and Management
Auburn University
Auburn, Alabama

Photographs ©: cover: Minden Pictures/Superstock, Inc.; 1: Alexsvirid/Dreamstime; 2-3 background: Carlos Neto/Dreamstime; 2-3 hippo: Alan Lucas/Dreamstime; 4, 5 background: robertharding/Superstock, Inc.; 5 top: MyImages-Micha/Shutterstock, Inc.; 5 bottom: trevor kittelty/Shutterstock, Inc.; 7: Image Source/Superstock, Inc.; 8: pavelp/iStockphoto; 11: Adwo/Shutterstock, Inc.; 12: Alan Lucas/Dreamstime; 15: Mat Hayward/Fotolia; 16: subin pumsom/Shutterstock, Inc.; 19: National News/ZUMAPRESS/Newscom; 20: Mint Images/Superstock, Inc.; 23: robertharding/Superstock, Inc.; 24: MyImages-Micha/Shutterstock, Inc.; 27: Animals Animals/Superstock, Inc.; 28: age fotostock/Alamy Images; 31: Tarker Archive/The Image Works; 32: Panoramic Images/Getty Images; 35: Francois Gohier/ardea.com/Pantheon/Superstock, Inc.; 36: trevor kittelty/Shutterstock, Inc.; 39: Rod/Getty Images; 40: Phyllis Greenberg/Animals Animals; 44-45 background: Carlos Neto/Dreamstime; 46: Alexsvirid/Dreamstime.

Map by Bob Italiano.

Library of Congress Cataloging-in-Publication Data
Names: Gregory, Josh, author.
Title: Hippopotamuses / by Josh Gregory.
Other titles: Nature's children (New York, N.Y.)
Description: New York : Children's Press, an imprint of Scholastic Inc.,
   [2017] | Series: Nature's children | Includes bibliographical references
   and index.
Identifiers: LCCN 2015043539| ISBN 9780531230275 (library
   binding : alk. paper) | ISBN 9780531219331 (pbk. : alk. paper)
Subjects: LCSH: Hippopotamus—Juvenile literature.
Classification: LCC QL737.U57 G747 2017 | DDC 599.63/5—dc23
LC record available at http://lccn.loc.gov/2015043539

No part of this publication may be reproduced in whole or in part, or stored in a retrieval system, or transmitted in any form or by any means, electronic, mechanical, photocopying, recording, or otherwise, without written permission of the publisher. For information regarding permission, write to Scholastic Inc., Attention: Permissions Department, 557 Broadway, New York, NY 10012.
© 2017 Scholastic Inc.

All rights reserved. Published in 2017 by Children's Press, an imprint of Scholastic Inc.

Printed in China 62
SCHOLASTIC, CHILDREN'S PRESS, and associated logos are trademarks and/or registered trademarks of Scholastic Inc.

1 2 3 4 5 6 7 8 9 10 R 26 25 24 23 22 21 20 19 18 17

Hippopotamuses

Class	Mammalia
Order	Artiodactyla
Family	Hippopotimidae
Genera	*Hippopotamus* and *Choeropsis*
Species	*Hippopotamus amphibius* and *Choeropsis liberiensis*
World distribution	Africa
Habitats	Common hippos live in rivers and lakes; pygmy hippos live in forests
Distinctive physical characteristics	Large, bulky bodies and very large heads; mouth can open up to 150 degrees; short, thick legs with four toes on each foot; common hippos weigh up to 3,252 pounds (1,475 kilograms); pygmy hippos weigh up to 542 pounds (246 kg); in both species, females are somewhat smaller than males; both species have gray skin with pinkish undersides; pygmy hippo is slightly darker in color; enormous teeth can grow up to 20 inches (51 centimeters) long in male common hippos
Habits	Spends most of the day sleeping half-submerged in water; leaves the water at night to graze for hours at a time; common hippos live together in large groups; pygmy hippos are usually either solitary or live in pairs; females reproduce once every two years; dominant males mate multiple times per year
Diet	Primarily grass; also eats leaves, fruit, and aquatic plants

Contents

CHAPTER 1

Rumble in the River

A narrow river runs through the middle of a forest in central Africa. Gathered in the water is a huge group of hippopotamuses. Most of the hippos' heads are visible above the surface of the river. Others bob up and down as they move about. It is early evening, and the enormous hippos are becoming more active after a day of napping. They are calm and peaceful.

In an instant, the situation changes. A strong male hippo has noticed a younger male approaching. As the young hippo nears, the older one springs into action. He opens his huge mouth as wide as possible to display the fearsome teeth inside. He splashes and roars. The younger hippo responds with a similar display. Enraged, the two hippos charge at each other. Other hippos scramble to get out of their way. The fight is on!

An angry hippo can be a frightening sight.

Massive Mammals

There are two hippopotamus **species** living today. The first one, the common hippo, also known as the river hippo, is familiar to most people. Weighing up to 3,252 pounds (1,475 kilograms), it can reach lengths of 16.4 feet (5 meters). This makes the species one of the largest land **mammals** on Earth. Only elephants are bigger. The common hippo has a huge round body and four short, thick legs. Its head is extremely large, and its tail is very short. Its skin is mostly gray with a pinkish shade on its underside.

The other species is called the pygmy hippo. Compared to a common hippo, it is small. But compared to most other animals, it is quite large. An adult male pygmy hippo can be up to 4.9 feet (1.5 m) long and weigh as much as 542 pounds (246 kg). Its skin is slightly darker than that of a common hippo.

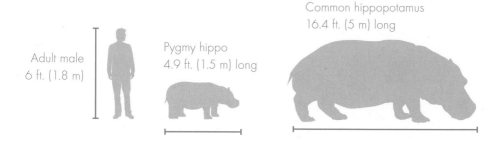

Common hippopotamus
16.4 ft. (5 m) long

Adult male
6 ft. (1.8 m)

Pygmy hippo
4.9 ft. (1.5 m) long

Pygmy hippos are much smaller than common hippos.

Hippo Homes

Wild hippos are found only in Africa. Common hippos live in many parts of the continent, especially in the central and eastern regions. A few live in the southern part of the continent. None are in the northern part. Pygmy hippos occupy a much smaller range of land. They are found mainly in the country of Liberia, in western Africa. For the most part, they do not live in the same areas as common hippos.

Common hippos are aquatic animals. This means they live only in areas where there is water. Hippos mostly like to live in and around rivers. They can also be found in lakes and swamps. A typical hippo habitat has plenty of grass and other plants growing nearby.

Pygmy hippos live in forests. These hippos do not spend as much time in the water as common hippos do. As a result, they do not need to live so close to rivers or lakes.

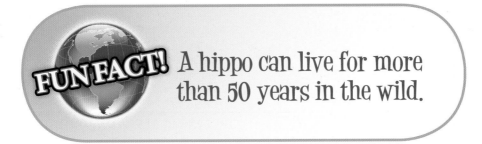

FUN FACT! A hippo can live for more than 50 years in the wild.

Water and grass are the main things a common hippo needs to survive.

CHAPTER 2

In Water and on Land

With their size, strength, and huge teeth, you might expect hippos to be deadly predators. However, these enormous animals are actually herbivores. Their diet is made up mostly of grass. Sometimes they also eat leaves or pieces of fruit that have fallen to the ground. In rivers and lakes, they might dive down to munch on underwater plants.

A hippo does not use its teeth when it is eating. Instead, it grips mouthfuls of grass with its strong lips to tear it from the ground. The hippo does not chew its food. It simply swallows the torn pieces of grass once they have been softened by saliva.

Each day, a hippo eats around 80 pounds (36 kg) of food. This might sound like a lot, but it actually isn't much for such a large animal. Because hippos spend so much time sitting still in water, they don't need much energy to live.

Grass is usually a hippo's main source of nutrition.

Aquatic Animals

As aquatic animals that spend more time in water than on land, common hippos have bodies that are very well suited to the aquatic lifestyle. A hippo's ears, eyes, and nostrils are all located on the top of its head. This enables the hippo to observe its surroundings while remaining almost entirely submerged. The hippo's senses are very sharp. Its sense of smell plays an important role in the animal's ability to navigate, find food, and communicate with other hippos. A hippo's hearing is also very good, even underwater.

When a hippo dives all the way underwater, it can fold its nostrils and ears shut to keep water from getting in. In addition, a hippo's eyes are protected with clear lenses. These act somewhat like swimming goggles, allowing the hippo to see very well underwater.

Hippos can hold their breath for five minutes or more when diving. They can even sleep underwater. A hippo has a special built-in reflex to return to the surface to breathe, without waking up.

Hippos are well suited to their aquatic lifestyle.

Resting and Running

There are a couple of reasons why hippos spend so much time in the water. If they spend too much time on land and in the sun, their skin can dry out quickly. They also become warm easily because they lack the ability to sweat. Diving into a river keeps a hippo cool, moist, and healthy.

Though it can't sweat, a hippo does have **glands** that release a pink, lotion-like substance to coat its skin. Scientists suspect that as this substance dries, it acts as a sort of sunblock. It might also protect the hippo from infections caused by swimming in dirty water.

Despite their aquatic lifestyle, hippos can't actually swim. Their bodies are too heavy and dense. Instead, they move through the water by using their toes to walk slowly along the sandy bottom. On land, they can move very fast for such large animals. When running, a hippo can reach speeds of 18.6 miles per hour (30 kilometers per hour).

A hippo can move around easily underwater.

Mighty Mouths

Due to its size and strength, a fully grown hippo faces few natural threats. The only predators that have any chance of taking down a hippo are powerful hunters such as lions, crocodiles, and hyenas. However, even these deadly animals tend to avoid hippos.

When they need to defend themselves, hippos are ferocious fighters. An adult hippo's mouth is about 1.6 feet (0.5 m) across and can open very wide. Inside are many large teeth. The longest of them can measure up to 20 inches (51 centimeters), and they are very sharp. One bite is all it takes for a hippo to cause tremendous damage.

Most of the fights hippos become involved in are against other hippos. When two of these animals clash, anything in their way can also be in danger. Smaller hippos are sometimes injured or killed by mistake when they end up in the middle of a brawl.

Even a lion is no match for a large adult hippo.

CHAPTER 3

Life in the Herd

A common hippo typically spends most or even all of the daylight hours resting in the water. This helps it stay out of the sun as it sleeps. Pygmy hippos, on the other hand, generally spend the day sleeping in a shady spot on land.

Hippos become much more active once the sun goes down. At night, they no longer have to worry about drying out or becoming too warm. They leave their resting places and travel to areas where they can graze. To reach them, hippos travel along paths that have been worn down over time by their heavy footsteps. A hippo's nightly grazing spot might be as far as 6 miles (9.7 km) from its daytime resting place. Once there, a hippo spends five or six hours eating before setting off on a return trip along the same path.

A hippo sniffs at a piece of fruit while looking for food at night.

Hippo Society

Common hippos live together in groups called herds. A herd is usually made up of about 10 to 15 hippos. However, the largest of these groups can have more than 100 members. Herd members protect one another from threats and share grazing areas. Aside from mothers and their offspring, hippos in a herd do not usually share very strong social bonds. Members can change frequently as hippos set off to live with different groups.

Pygmy hippos are not as social as their larger cousins. They are often solitary animals. Other times, they might travel together in pairs.

Hippos tell each other apart by scent. Their sense of smell also helps them follow one another to grazing areas when it is dark outside. Hippos communicate using a wide range of sounds as well. When they are angry, they can roar at the same volume as a rock concert. They can also make snorting, honking, clicking, and wheezing sounds, among others.

Rivers can get very crowded during the day when a large hippo herd is in the water.

Tussling over Territory

Hippos do not always get along peacefully. Adult males, or bulls, are very territorial. They claim areas of water called mating territories. They do not allow other males to mate with the female hippos, or cows, in these areas. A bull might control a certain territory for many years at a time. To protect the boundary of his territory, a bull will face off against the dominant males in neighboring areas. Two bulls meet face-to-face at these borders and stare each other down as they lift their rear ends into the air. They then use their tails to spray urine and feces all around themselves, marking their territory.

When a bull thinks another male is trying to mate with the females in his territory, he first tries to intimidate the rival. He roars, opens his mouth wide, and splashes around. He might even charge forward. If the rival is not frightened away, the bull might attack. One of the males is often injured or killed in these bursts of violence.

Hippos can be extremely vicious when defending their territory.

Mating Season

Hippos tend to mate during the driest time of the year, roughly from February to August. This ensures that babies are born during the rainier period, when there is plenty of food and water.

A hippo cow mates about once every two years. When she is ready to mate, her body gives off a special scent. When the bull that controls the mating territory detects this scent, he approaches her and mates with her. The bull mates many times each year, depending on how many cows are in his territory.

A common hippo's gestation period lasts about eight months. When a cow is ready to give birth, she leaves the herd to find a more private place. This gives her space to form a strong bond with her new baby. She returns to the group once the baby is about two weeks old.

A pygmy hippo's gestation is a little shorter, usually six to seven months. Because she does not live with a herd, she already has plenty of space to bond with her baby.

A mother hippo helps her baby out of the water.

Big Babies

A newborn common hippo weighs about 100 pounds (45.4 kg). Despite its large size, it is vulnerable to predators. Its mother goes several days without eating so she can remain near her baby and protect it. Pygmy hippos are born much smaller, at 10 to 13.5 pounds (4.5 to 6 kg). When the mother has to eat, she hides the baby nearby in bushes or brush.

A baby hippo eats by drinking milk from its mother's body. When a mother common hippo is in the water, the baby swims beneath her to reach the milk. A baby common hippo can move easily in the water as soon as it is born. It automatically knows to close its ears and nose when diving. To rest, it might climb on its mother's back. Once it is about a month old, it begins eating grass. When the young hippo is about six to eight months old, it stops drinking milk completely. However, it does not reach adulthood until it is 6 to 15 years old.

FUN FACT! Common hippos can give birth either on land or in the water.

A young hippo takes a break from swimming by resting on its mother's back.

CHAPTER 4

Ancestors and Relatives

Hippos have existed for a very long time. Scientists have uncovered fossils of animals very similar to today's pygmy hippos. Those fossils date from 23 million to 16 million years ago. Since then, hippos have gone through many changes. Some became extinct. Others developed into the animals we know today.

The hippo's early ancestors probably traveled to Africa from Asia about 35 million years ago. These animals changed over time to become more like modern hippos. They also spread into other parts of the world. Thousands of years ago, hippos could be found throughout all of Africa. They even lived in parts of Europe and Asia. Because of hunting and changes in climate, however, hippos died out in many places. This eventually reduced their range to its present-day size.

Ancient Egyptians created artwork based on the hippos they saw in African rivers.

Hippos and Pigs

One animal that shares ancestors with hippos is the pig. There are many types of pigs living today. Like hippos, they have large, round bodies, short legs and tails, and big heads. While the largest pigs can weigh hundreds of pounds, none are quite as big as their hippo relatives.

Like hippos, pigs have long, tusklike teeth that they often use as weapons. Hippos and pigs also have similar ridges on their back teeth. These commonalities are some of the main clues scientists used to determine that the two animals are related.

Today, pigs are found in many parts of the world. Wild species are known as boars. There are several varieties of **domestic** pigs as well. These animals are an important source of meat for many people.

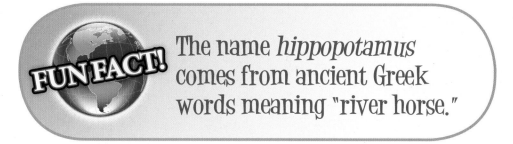

FUN FACT! The name *hippopotamus* comes from ancient Greek words meaning "river horse."

Warthogs, a type of pig, share many physical similarities with their hippo relatives.

Aquatic Cousins

For years, scientists believed that the pig was the hippo's closest living relative. However, recent studies have uncovered evidence that hippos are even more closely related to whales. Fossils show hippo ancestors called anthracotheres lived around 30 million years ago. Like today's hippos, these animals probably spent time both on land and in water. By studying anthracothere fossils, scientists determined that the animals were close relatives of ancient whales. These ancient whales had legs and lived on land.

Like hippos, modern whales have thick, mostly hairless skin and can be very large. In fact, the blue whale is believed to be the largest animal ever to live on Earth. Blue whales can reach lengths of 100 feet (30.5 m). The heaviest blue whale ever recorded weighed 198.4 tons. That is far heavier than even the largest known dinosaur species.

A young blue whale breaches the surface of the water in the Gulf of California.

CHAPTER 5

Hippos and Humans

For humans, being up close and personal with a hippo is often a terrifying and dangerous experience. Hippos are not normally aggressive toward people. However, hippo attacks do happen. Sometimes hippos might mistake a boat for an approaching crocodile. Other times, humans stumble upon them and catch the animals off guard. Mother hippos become aggressive if people get too close to their babies. In such situations, hippos lash out reflexively to protect themselves and their fellow herd members.

If attacked by a hippo, a human is likely to suffer severe injuries or even be killed. As a result, people who live where hippos are found consider them more dangerous than any other animal. Some experts estimate that hippos kill more people every year than do all other wild African animals combined.

As they work, fishermen in Africa must be careful not to disturb hippos.

Hunted Hippos

As dangerous as meeting a hippo is, humans cause far more damage to these animals than hippos cause humans. In many parts of Africa, hippos are slowly disappearing from the wild. In the past, many farmers killed hippos to keep them from damaging crops. Such killings played a major role in eliminating hippos from northern Africa. More recently, experts estimate that as many as 20 percent of all wild hippos may have been wiped out between 1998 and 2008. There are few signs of this problem slowing down. Pygmy hippos are especially at risk. They are listed as an endangered species.

One major reason for the decline in the hippo population is poaching. Hippos are often killed for their teeth, which are made of ivory. This valuable material has been used to create everything from piano keys to statues. Poachers can also make money by selling meat and skins from hippos.

Poachers in Uganda and other African countries sometimes kill hippos for their meat.

Harm to Habitats

Habitat loss is another major issue affecting the survival of hippos. The world's human population is always increasing. As the number of people grows, more space is needed for them to live. More resources are used to create the everyday items people consume. As a result, wildland is cleared to make room for settlements and farms. Trees are cut down to make wood and paper products. This leaves hippos and other wild animals with less space to live. It also makes it easier for poachers to reach areas that may once have been surrounded by dense forests.

Governments have passed laws to help protect hippos from poachers. They have also set aside areas of land that cannot be cleared for human use. However, it will take more than this to ensure that hippos remain a part of our world. Only by paying careful attention to these fascinating creatures and respecting their needs can we preserve them and their natural environment.

Protecting wild habitats is an important part of keeping hippos safe and healthy.

Words to Know

ancestors (AN-ses-turz) — ancient animal species that are related to modern species

aquatic (uh-KWAH-tik) — living or growing in water

climate (KLYE-mit) — the weather typical of a place over a long period of time

domestic (duh-MES-tik) — animals that have been tamed; people use them as a source of food or as work animals, or keep them as pets

endangered (en-DAYN-jurd) — at risk of becoming extinct, usually because of human activity

extinct (ik-STINGKT) — no longer found alive

fossils (FAH-suhlz) — the hardened remains of prehistoric plants and animals

gestation (jes-TAY-shun) — the time during which a baby develops inside its mother before being born

glands (GLANDZ) — organs in the body that produce or release natural chemicals

graze (GRAYZ) — to feed on grass or other plants

habitat (HAB-uh-tat) — the place where an animal or a plant is usually found herbivores (HUR-buh-vorz) — animals that only eat plants

mammals (MAM-uhlz) — warm-blooded animals that have hair or fur and usually give birth to live young

mate (MAYT) — to join together to produce babies

poaching (POH-ching) — hunting or fishing illegally

predators (PREH-duh-turz) — animals that live by hunting other animals for food

solitary (SAH-lih-ter-ee) — preferring to live alone

species (SPEE-sheez) — one of the groups into which animals and plants of the same genus are divided

territorial (terr-uh-TOR-ee-uhl) — defensive of a certain area

Habitat Map

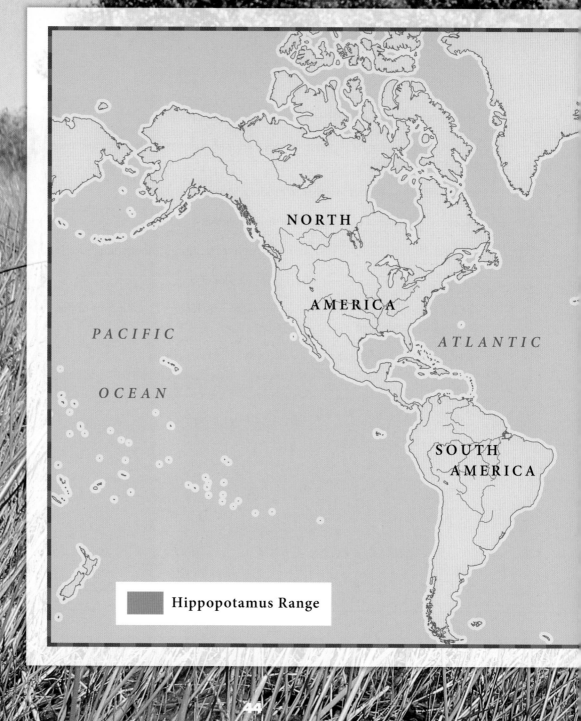

NORTH

AMERICA

PACIFIC

OCEAN

ATLANTIC

SOUTH
AMERICA

Hippopotamus Range

ARCTIC OCEAN

EUROPE

ASIA

AFRICA

PACIFIC OCEAN

OCEAN

INDIAN

OCEAN

AUSTRALIA

Find Out More

Books

Clarke, Penny. *Hippos*. New York: Franklin Watts, 2009.

Gish, Melissa. *Hippopotamuses*. Mankato, MN: Creative Paperbacks, 2014.

Smith, Luck Sackett. *Hippos: Huge and Hungry*. New York: PowerKids Press, 2010.

Visit this Scholastic Web site for more information on hippopotamuses:
www.factsfornow.scholastic.com
Enter the keyword **Hippopotamuses**

Index

Page numbers in *italics* indicate a photograph or map.

About the Author

Josh Gregory is the author of more than 90 books
for kids. He has written about everything from
animals to technology to history. A graduate of the
University of Missouri-Columbia, he currently lives
in Portland, Oregon.